Contents

Contents

VOL 1
CLIMATE
CHRONICLES
WHY IS THE EARTH
FEELING WARMER?
MOONSTONE

Published in Moonstone
by Rupa Publications India Pvt. Ltd 2024
7/16, Ansari Road, Daryaganj
New Delhi 110002

Sales centres:
Bengaluru Chennai
Hyderabad Jaipur Kathmandu
Kolkata Mumbai Prayagraj

P-ISBN: 978-93-6156-755-1
E-ISBN: 978-93-6156-002-6

First impression 2024

10 9 8 7 6 5 4 3 2 1

Printed in India

CLIMATE CHANGE

Introduction

Climate refers to the average weather pattern of an area, while weather is the current state of the atmosphere in a specific region, influenced by factors like rainfall, temperature, air pressure, and humidity. Weather changes daily. Climate change, however, is a complex phenomenon with significant ecological consequences.

Global temperature rise over decades confirms climate change, largely driven by human activities. Adapting to these changes is challenging but necessary. To mitigate further damage, individuals must adopt a responsible attitude toward nature and curb activities harming it in the long term.

Climate in the Past

Around 2.7 billion years ago, Earth's first ice age occurred, covering everything in thick ice sheets. Subsequent warming followed until another ice age approximately 850 million years ago. The most recent ice age ended around 11,000 years ago, marking the start of the current period, the Holocene Epoch.

The Younger Dryas

The earth's temperature began to rise around 14,500 years ago, transitioning from glacial to interglacial conditions. However, the climate reverted to glacial conditions for a brief period. This period is known as the Younger Dryas. It lasted for approximately 1,200 to 1,300 years and occurred between 12,800 and 11,500 years ago.

The Younger Dryas cooling

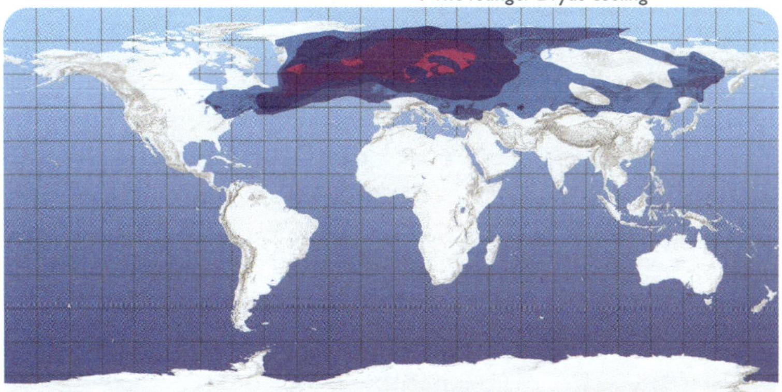

FUN FACT

The Younger Dryas obtained its name from a flower known as Dryas octopetala, which thrives in cold climates.

8.2 Kiloyear Event

The Earth's temperature rose during the Holocene Period, but about 8,200 years ago, there was an abrupt climate change, causing a cooling period lasting two to four centuries. Scientists refer to this as the 8.2 kiloyear event.

The Little Ice Age

Between the 16th and mid-19th centuries, global temperatures were about 3°F colder than today. This led to widespread famine and agricultural struggles, along with violent storms causing the loss of life. Despite the cold, it wasn't classified as an ice age as it didn't last long enough for ice sheets to expand.

? What is the present period called? ______________________

Greenhouse Effect

When sunlight touches Earth, it's not a one-way trip. Greenhouse gases in the atmosphere grab hold of some of the outgoing radiation, creating a warming effect. Think of them as nature's cosy blanket, ensuring our planet stays warm enough to support life. This captivating process is aptly named the greenhouse effect.

Carbon Cycle

CO_2 plays a vital role in supporting life on Earth. Humans and animals exhale CO_2 during respiration, which plants then absorb during photosynthesis, releasing oxygen. This carbon cycle maintains CO_2 balance. However, human activities like burning fossil fuels, deforestation, and pollution release additional CO_2, increasing atmospheric carbon levels. This contributes to rising temperatures and global climate change.

Greenhouse Gases

Water vapour, nitrous oxide, CO_2, ozone (O_3), and methane (CH4) are natural greenhouse gases. Chlorofluorocarbons (CFCs) are man-made. Human activities, including industrialisation, have significantly increased levels of these gases in the atmosphere. Emissions from airplanes, fires, and local pollution also contribute to the greenhouse effect.

FUN FACT

The Mauna Loa Observatory (MLO) in Hawaii monitors and collects data about atmospheric carbon dioxide.

? The greenhouse effect has a bad effect on earth. (True/False)

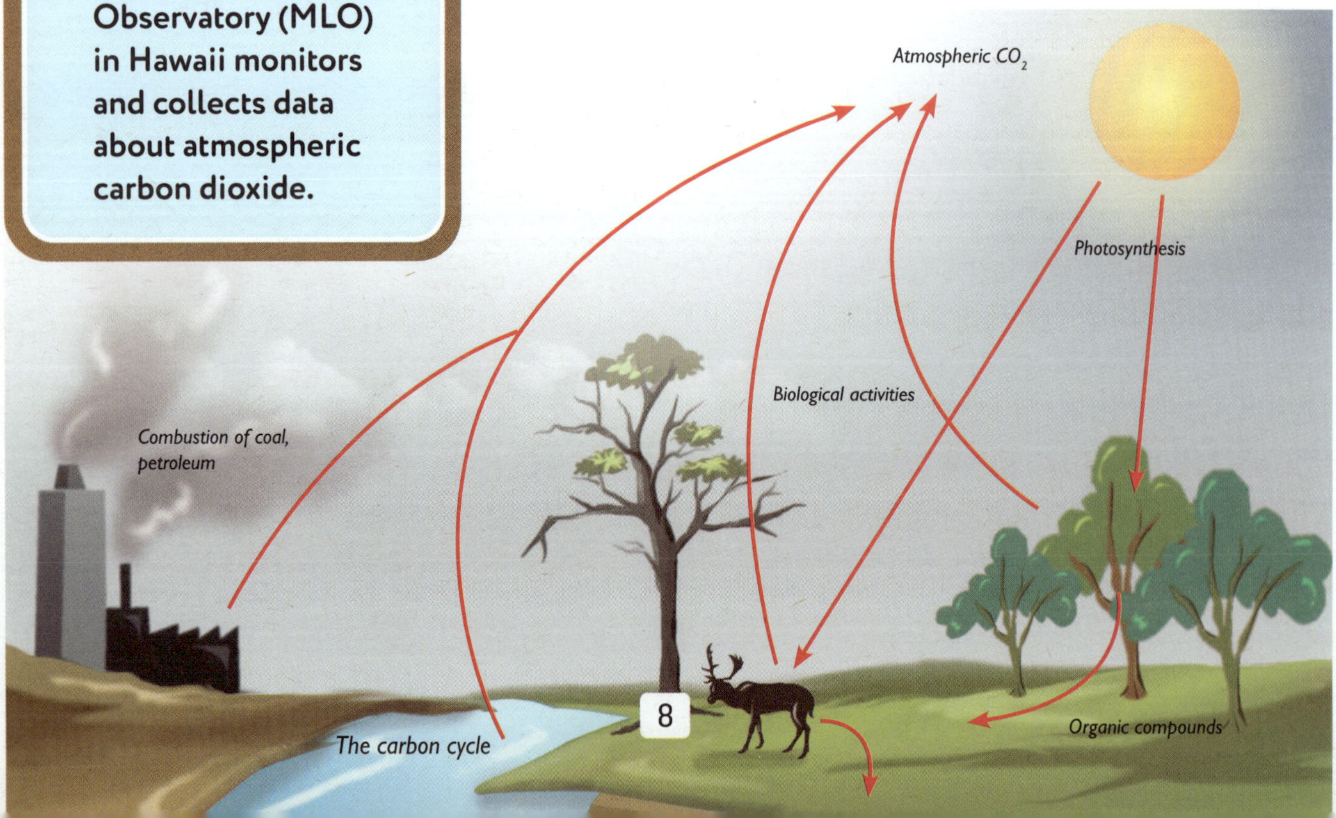

The carbon cycle

The Ozone Hole

Ozone (O_3) naturally occurs in Earth's atmosphere, alongside other gases. It plays a crucial role by absorbing about 90 percent of harmful Ultraviolet B Radiation (UVB) from the sun, acting as a shield for living beings. Excessive UVB exposure can lead to skin diseases like skin cancer in humans and contribute to glacial melting.

The Ozone Hole

In the 1970s, scientists observed the depletion of the ozone layer over the South Pole. Man-made greenhouse gases (GHGs) like CFCs from refrigerators, halons from fire extinguishers, and hydrochlorofluorocarbons (HCFCs) are responsible for this ozone loss. When these gases reach the stratosphere, UV rays break them down, releasing chlorine atoms. Just one chlorine atom can destroy 100,000 ozone molecules, resulting in significant damage to the ozone layer.

Arctic Ozone Hole

In 2011, scientists confirmed that long-lasting, extreme cold conditions and the surge of ozone-depleting substances caused the formation of an ozone hole over the Arctic. Cooling of the ozone layer in the Arctic increases the effect of CFCs, which destroy the ozone.

FUN FACT

By 2050, the ozone layer is predicted to fully heal due to a drastic reduction in ozone-depleting substances.

Tibet Ozone Hole

In 2006, research confirmed a 2.5 million-square-kilometre hole in the low-level ozone layer over China's Qinghai-Tibet Plateau. By 2011, an ozone hole had formed over mountainous regions including Tibet, Xinxiang, Qinghai, and the Hindu Kush.

? What do CFCs stand for? ____________________

The Montreal Protocol

Signed by 46 United Nations members, the Montreal Protocol is an international treaty aimed at gradually reducing ozone-depleting substances and replacing them with ozone-friendly alternatives. Opened for signatures on September 16, 1987, the treaty came into effect on January 1, 1989.

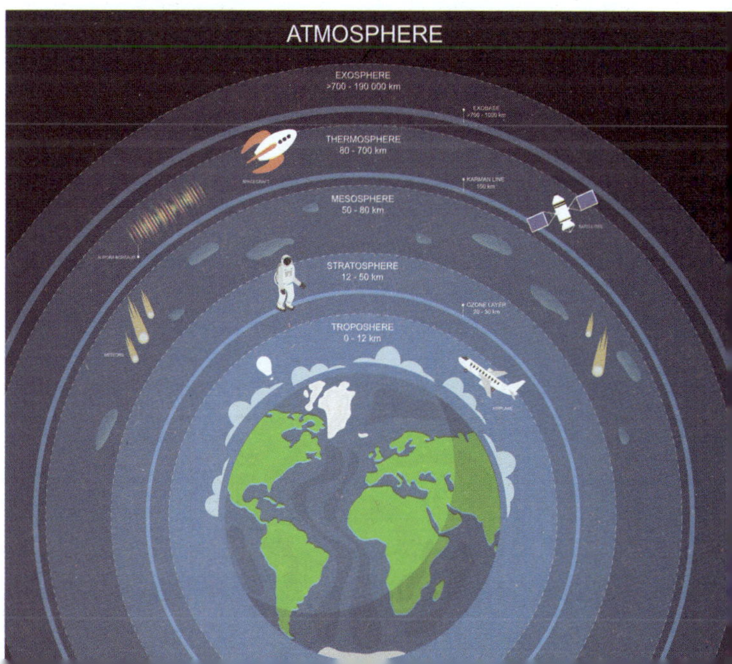

Natural Causes

Climate change arises from both man-made and natural causes. While natural factors may not prompt drastic climate shifts, they have a lasting impact. Millions of years ago, as landmasses drifted to shape today's continents, they altered ocean currents, thereby influencing the global climate.

Earth's Orbit

Every few thousand years, variations in the Earth's tilt and orbit directly influence its climate, causing significant changes in seasonal patterns. Even slight alterations in the Earth's axial tilt can lead to drastic shifts, potentially resulting in warmer summers or colder winters. Changes in the Earth's orbit, occurring approximately every 100,000 years, and its axial tilt, happening roughly every 41,000 years, directly affect the amount of sunlight reaching the Earth's surface, triggering dramatic climate shifts like ice ages. These insights originated with Milutin Milanković, a Serbian mathematician.

Solar Variation

Every 11 years, the sun's activity cycles from stormy to quiet phases and vice versa due to concentrated magnetic fields. During solar maximum, when solar activity is high, solar radiation measurements increase, while solar irradiance decreases. This leads to a slight temperature change of about 0.1°C on Earth, with temperatures slightly warmer during solar maximum and cooler during solar minimum.

FUN FACT

The 1991 eruption of Mt. Pinatubo released 20 million tonnes of sulphur, cooling the lower troposphere for two years.

? Seasons are caused due to the tilt of earth's ________.

El Niño and La Niña

El Niño–Southern Oscillation (ENSO) is a natural climate pattern recurring every 5 to 8 years near the Pacific Ocean. It leads to elevated sea surface temperatures near the equator. Conversely, during La Niña events, temperatures in the same area drop below normal levels. Both phenomena significantly impact climate patterns worldwide.

Effect of El Niño

During El Niño events, the northern hemisphere experiences heavy rainfall in southern America, leading to floods from Ecuador to the Gulf of Mexico, and hurricanes in Hawaii and Tahiti. Simultaneously, it causes severe droughts in areas like Central America and Australia, and warmer winters in the eastern US.

Global warming and Weather Events

Global warming disrupts ocean currents and weather systems, hindering the release of excess heat from tropical seas. Warmer ocean temperatures have intensified and increased the frequency of El Niño and La Niña events in recent decades. This leads to heightened evaporation from land and increased moisture in the air, intensifying storms and floods associated with El Niño.

FUN FACT

The severe drought caused by the 1876 El Niño is estimated to have killed 18 million people across India and China.

Effect of La Niña

La Niña events counteract the impacts of El Niño. They bring droughts to Southern America and widespread floods and rainfall to eastern Australia. Winters become colder and drier than usual during La Niña periods. Marine animals benefit from La Niña as deep-seated nutrients are brought to the surface by ocean currents, providing abundant food.

? ENSO stands for ________________.

Human Influences

Human actions significantly fuel global warming by emitting potent greenhouse gases such as CO_2 and methane, intensifying the greenhouse effect. These gases vary in their heat-trapping abilities. Consequently, human activities bear partial responsibility for altering the Earth's climate.

Deforestation

Industrial expansion has led to widespread deforestation, with trees being increasingly cut down for various industries such as wood and paper production without sufficient reforestation efforts. This massive deforestation has raised the levels of CO_2 in the atmosphere. With fewer trees to absorb this excess CO_2, the greenhouse effect is amplified, exacerbating the global warming trend.

FUN FACT

According to Carbon Brief, human emissions and activities have caused around 100% of the warming observed.

Overpopulation

Rapid population growth drives excessive consumption of fossil fuels to fulfill human requirements. These fuels power electricity generation, transportation, and industrial operations, resulting in vast CO_2 emissions. Approximately three-quarters of human-caused CO_2 emissions stem from these activities.

? Deforestation does not affect the carbon cycle. (True/False)

Industrial Emissions

Since the Industrial Revolution began in the 1800s, there's been a significant surge in greenhouse gases in the atmosphere. Industries and transportation are primarily to blame for the rise in CO_2 levels. Over the past 150 years, CO_2 concentrations have increased from 280 to 379 parts per million (ppm) due to industrial emissions. In the United States alone, vehicles contribute approximately 1.7 billion tonnes of CO_2 annually.

Deaths and Diseases

Climate change presents a significant threat to human health. Rising global temperatures are challenging human adaptation to atmospheric shifts, leading to an escalation in heat-related illnesses and diseases. Despite efforts to adapt, the rapid pace of climate change introduces new health challenges.

Illnesses and Deaths

Rising temperatures have led to an increase in heat-related illnesses, including heatstroke, heat cramps, high body temperatures, and heat exhaustion. Extreme heat can be fatal, with infants, elderly individuals, and those with preexisting conditions particularly vulnerable. Between 1998 and 2011, approximately 500 children died from heatstroke in the US during the summer months.

Climate-sensitive Diseases

Climate change is increasing the spread of vector-borne diseases, particularly those found in warmer regions and transmitted by mosquitoes and other insects. Deadly diseases such as malaria, dengue fever, and yellow fever are on the rise. Additionally, the increase in rainfall and temperature extends the period for disease transmission.

Respiratory Problems

Climate change increases smog (ground-level ozone), which contains harmful particles causing severe damage to the respiratory system upon inhalation. It reduces lung capacity and worsens asthma. High temperatures also lead to an early start to the pollen season. The allergenic pollen produced by weedy plant species further increases discomfort for people with respiratory disorders.

? Heatwaves can cause death. (True/False)

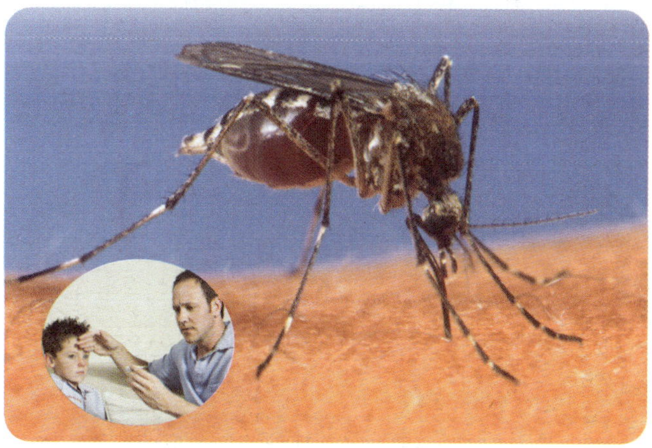

FUN FACT

According to the United Nations, environmental factors kill around 13 million people every year.

Natural Disasters

Natural disasters like tsunamis, hurricanes, earthquakes, floods, and heatwaves were once rare but have become more frequent due to climate change. The Rio de Janeiro floods (2011), Japan earthquake and tsunami (2012), Nepal earthquake (2015), and UK heatwave (2011) are all linked to climate change.

Heatwaves

James Hansen, a leading US scientist, recently suggested that the deadly European heatwave of 2003 and the Russian heatwave of 2010 can both be linked to climate change and global warming. Studies repeatedly indicate that heatwaves have increased in recent years due to rising temperatures. Furthermore, changes in rainfall patterns are identified as an indicator of impending heatwaves.

Floods and Droughts

As temperatures rise, so does the amount of water vapour in the atmosphere, leading to higher levels of precipitation. In some areas, heavy rainfall raises water levels in rivers and lakes, causing extreme floods. However, other regions experience reduced rainfall, resulting in severe droughts. This dryness renders lands barren, causing water resources such as rivers, lakes, and ponds to dry up.

FUN FACT

The longest recorded dry period was 14.33 years, from October 10, 1903 to January 1, 1918, in Arica, Chile.

Hurricanes

Hurricanes are tropical storms that form when ocean water warms up, evaporates, and combines with strong winds. They derive their energy from the warming oceans. With oceans heating up due to climate change, the frequency of severe hurricanes is increasing.

? Are hurricanes tropical storms?

____

Impact on Agriculture

Agriculture heavily relies on climatic conditions. Warmer temperatures disrupt the production of certain crops and promote the growth of weeds and pests. Changes in precipitation patterns also lead to crop failures. While humans are developing new technologies to enhance crop productivity, climate change poses a significant obstacle.

Changing Crop Seasons

The increasing temperature significantly impacts crop growth in regions with persistent high temperatures, such as California, where wine grape production is declining. Conversely, crop production in cold climatic regions like the Great Lakes region and Canada is increasing due to an extended growth season.

CO_2 Fertilisation

Although CO2 is a greenhouse gas, it benefits the agricultural sector by acting as a fertiliser, enhancing the production of crops like soybeans, rice, and wheat in regions with higher atmospheric CO2 concentrations. This process, known as CO2 fertilisation, is affected by climate change, which can alter the availability of water and nutrients essential for crop growth.

FUN FACT

Annually, about 3.5 million people die worldwide due to the malnutrition caused by droughts.

Changing Rainfall Patterns

Climate change alters precipitation patterns significantly. Areas near water bodies experience increased rainfall due to higher evaporation rates, while remote areas suffer from droughts caused by intensified soil evaporation. This adversely affects soil quality and crop production.

? CO_2 fertilisation helps in crop growth. (True/False)

Impact on Wildlife

Global warming and climate change are impacting wildlife by necessitating habitat and migration pattern adjustments. Numerous species are now under the threat of extinction. Climate change disrupts animal life cycles, reproduction rates, timing, and feeding behaviours.

Mammals

Mammals worldwide are witnessing shifts in their breeding and hibernation behaviours. These changes are attributed to increasing temperatures, reduced food availability, and alterations in lifestyle. Polar bears, which rely on floating ice for hunting, and seals, which birth, nurse, and rest their young on snow, are particularly endangered by the melting summer sea ice.

Birds

Migratory birds now make early stops in colder regions due to warmer climates, initiating early breeding and nesting. However, their early arrival does not ensure the availability of insects, crucial for their food supply. Similar situations affect other bird species.

Early onset of summer may affect the flight pattern of migratory birds like the Arctic tern.

Fish and Amphibians

Rising temperatures affect water quality, impacting fish and amphibian productivity and diversity. For instance, in high winter temperatures, the eggs of coldwater species like yellow perch do not survive. Many salamander and frog species lay eggs in pools formed after snowmelt, but these dry out in hot weather, affecting population growth.

FUN FACT

The Bramble Cay melomys (Melomys rubicola) is the first mammal reported to have gone extinct as a direct result of climate change.

?

Polar bears are not affected by global warming. (True/False)

Impact on Coral Reefs

Coral reefs, built from calcium carbonate by shellfish, coralline algae, and corals, host a quarter of the world's marine life, provide coastal storm protection, and are a major tourist draw.

Coral Bleaching

Corals rely on zooxanthellae algae for colour and food through photosynthesis, while corals provide shelter and light. Warmer temperatures are causing corals to expel these algae, resulting in coral bleaching, where the colonies lose colour and expose white calcium carbonate structures.

Great Barrier Reef Bleaching (1997-98)

The 1997-98 El Niño weather events raised the temperature of the Great Barrier Reef in Australia by approximately 2°C, resulting in extensive coral bleaching. Around 87 percent of inshore reefs experienced some degree of bleaching. If ocean temperatures continue to increase, it is estimated that the Great Barrier Reef could lose up to 95 percent of its corals by 2050.

FUN FACT

According to the "Status of Coral Reefs of the World: 2020" report, the world has lost around 14% of its coral since 2009.

Great Barrier Reef Bleaching (2023)

According to a 2023 report, the Great Barrier Reef has recorded less than 10% coral bleaching in 2023. The report also states that no reefs have been bleached in 2023.

? What type of algae is in coral? ____________________

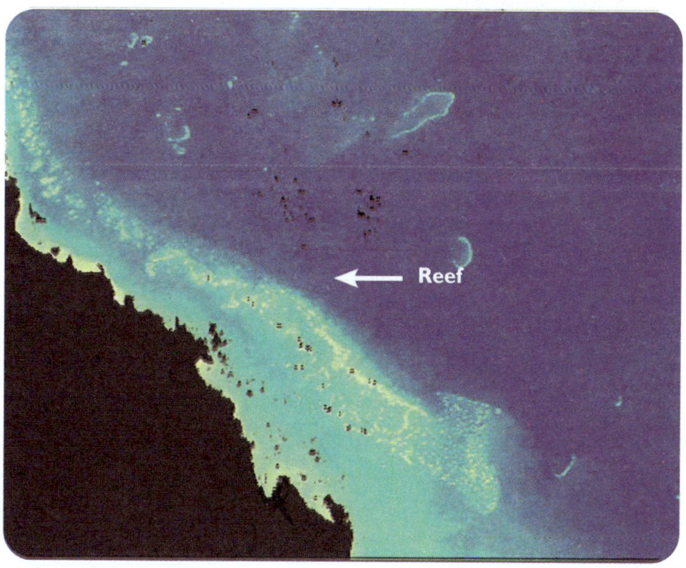

Impact on Forests

After the last ice age, trees adapted to a temperature rise of about 2-3°C. However, global temperatures are projected to increase by 1.5-5.8°C before the end of this century. Adapting to such rapid climate change would significantly impact forests worldwide. Forests and their soils store over one trillion tonnes of carbon, twice the amount in the atmosphere.

Changes in Growth

High temperatures are reducing the growth and productivity of boreal forests in high-altitude regions. Tropical forests, on the other hand, are already adapted to high temperatures. In temperate regions, forests are transitioning to new species better suited to changing climates. In areas experiencing decreased precipitation due to climate change, forests are dying out and being replaced by shrubs and grasslands.

Economic Effect

Predictions suggest that forest productivity in the US could rise due to climate change, potentially leading to increased timber production and lower timber prices in the future. Additionally, outdoor camps offering activities such as fishing, hiking, hunting, and camping may benefit from the expansion of forests.

FUN FACT

Every day, over 1000 children under 5 die from diseases linked to inadequate water, sanitation and hygiene.

Forest Fires

Rising temperatures are making soils and trees drier, leading to more lightning and increasing the risk of forest fires. Additionally, climate change is boosting insect and pest populations, resulting in the destruction of millions of trees globally. These factors are impeding forest growth and putting pressure on ecosystems.

? Forests in the high-altitude regions are called ________.

Impact on Waterbodies

One significant consequence of global warming is the reduction in freshwater bodies caused by high rates of evaporation. Additionally, it contributes to the accelerated melting of polar ice, resulting in rising sea levels and affecting marine water quality. The water cycle, a vital natural process, is also experiencing disruptions.

Ocean Acidification

Oceans absorb approximately one-third of atmospheric CO_2, depositing it in the deep where it forms carbonic acid, thereby increasing ocean acidity. This acidification will significantly impact the marine ecosystem, with certain species facing survival challenges as it worsens.

FUN FACT

According to the United Nations, approximately two billion people worldwide lack access to safe drinking water, while roughly half of the global population faces severe water scarcity for at least part of the year.

Rise in sea levels

Sea levels are rising due to two primary factors. Firstly, the warming of the oceans leads to the expansion of seawater. Secondly, the melting of glaciers and sea ice from Antarctica and Greenland contributes to the increase. This rise poses a significant threat to approximately two-thirds of the world's coastal cities.

Glaciers and Ice Sheets

Glaciers, slow-moving rivers of ice, cover about 10 percent of the Earth's land area and are the largest reservoirs of fresh water. However, rising temperatures are rapidly melting them, causing a loss of ice mass. For example, Mount Kilimanjaro's glacial ice in Africa has decreased by 80 percent in the last century.

? Melting glaciers are increasing the _____ level.

Impact on Drinking Water

Despite 75 percent of the Earth being covered with water, there is a shortage of drinking water. Only about 1.2 percent of the Earth's water is drinkable, with most of it locked in the ice sheets of Antarctica and Greenland. This leaves a limited amount for drinking and agricultural purposes. Rapid climate changes are further impacting the availability of drinking water.

More Demand, Less Supply

Currently, one-fifth of the global population faces water shortages, with water usage doubling the rate of population growth. In about 75 percent of Chinese cities, demand exceeds supply, while Africa experiences year-round water scarcity. Climate change is reducing freshwater sources, including shrinking glaciers in the Himalayas.

Saltwater Intrusion

As sea levels rise due to global warming, there is a risk of saline water from seas infiltrating coastal freshwater aquifers. Furthermore, groundwater in these aquifers is depleting faster than it can recharge, potentially leading to future shortages of drinking water.

FUN FACT

Every day, over 1000 children under 5 die from diseases linked to inadequate water, sanitation and hygiene.

? What percentage of the earth's water is drinkable? __________

Low Quality of Water

Increasing temperatures result in more precipitation, but this does not necessarily translate to an increase in potable water. While freshwater bodies are naturally cleansed by certain organisms, warm water leads to decreased oxygen content, affecting their populations. Moreover, excessive rainfall causes harmful contaminants from land to runoff into rivers, rendering the water unfit for drinking. During extreme rainfall, municipal sewer systems may overflow, leading to untreated sewage entering drinking water supplies.

Polar Regions

The Arctic Circle in the northern hemisphere and the Antarctic Circle in the southern hemisphere are the polar regions. While the Arctic is a frozen ocean surrounded by land, Antarctica is an ice-covered continent. The Arctic is warming 2.5 times faster than the global average. Alaska has gotten about 3.4 degrees Fahrenheit warmer on average.

The Arctic Ice Melt

Ice reflects more sunlight than ocean or land, increasing Earth's sunlight absorption as Arctic ice melts, contributing to global warming. Melting glaciers elevate sea levels, impacting coastal communities. Biodiversity suffers as migratory birds rely heavily on Arctic regions for feeding and breeding. Polar bears and several seal species face extinction threats.

Antarctica

Climate change impacts Antarctica unevenly. While sea ice is growing in certain regions, it's rapidly shrinking elsewhere, impacting wildlife. Declining krill populations, which feed on algae under sea ice, affect Adélie penguins that rely on krill for food. Over the last 50 years, the region's temperature has risen by approximately 3° C, with around 60 billion tonnes of ice mass lost in 2006 alone.

FUN FACT

The oldest and thickest Arctic sea ice has declined by 95% over the past 30 years. Arctic sea ice is shrinking at a rate of almost 13% per decade.

? Can polar ice reflect sunrays?

____

International Treaties

Multiple nations have united to combat climate change through treaties aimed at curbing pollution and greenhouse gas emissions. Developed and industrialized nations, like the US, being major GHG producers, bear significant responsibility for environmental preservation.

UNFCCC

The United Nations Framework Convention on Climate Change (UNFCCC) was signed by approximately 150 countries in June 1992 in Rio de Janeiro, Brazil, and enforced in March 1994. Its primary aim is to regulate greenhouse gas (GHG) levels in the atmosphere to mitigate the impact of human activities on the global climate system. However, the treaty lacks binding limits on emissions from any nation.

COP 15

In December 2009, the 15th Conference of the Parties of UNFCCC convened in Copenhagen, Denmark, seeking a post-Kyoto Protocol solution for global climate change. Despite efforts, only a non-binding agreement was reached by China, Brazil, India, South Africa, and the US, acknowledging the need to limit temperature increase to 2°C. However, it did not impose caps on CO_2 emissions from participating countries.

Kyoto Protocol

In December 1997, the Kyoto Protocol was signed in Kyoto, Japan, and enforced in February 2005. This protocol mandated that by 2012, 37 industrialised nations reduce their emissions of methane, sulfur hexafluoride, carbon dioxide, hydrofluorocarbons, and nitrous oxide by 5.2 percent.

FUN FACT

The Montreal Protocol has succeeded in eliminating nearly 99 percent of these ozone-depleting substances.

? The full form of UNFCCC is ______.

Climate in the Future

Predicting future climate change is challenging due to uncertainties in curbing emissions to stabilize global temperatures. Given the present circumstances, the Intergovernmental Panel on Climate Change (IPCC), tasked with assessing global climate data, has made projections regarding potential climatic impacts.

Rise in GHGs

GHG emissions are increasing, and the IPCC predicts a 41 to 158 percent rise in CO_2 concentration by 2100, depending on the location.

Rising Temperature

The IPCC projects that by 2100, the global average surface temperature will increase by 2° to 11.5°F, compared to 3.2° to 7.2°F during 1980-90. Warmer conditions are expected near the Arctic Circle due to increased sunlight absorption by melted Arctic ice.

Rising Sea Levels

The IPCC predicts that by 2100, the average global sea level may rise by 7.2 to 23.6 inches, excluding ice sheet flow. This projection considers the 0.17-metre global average sea level rise observed in the twentieth century.

? The full form of IPCC is ____________________.

FUN FACT

Global average temperature is expected to warm at least twice as much in the next 100 years as it has during the last 100 years.

Adaptation

Climate change remains a continuous phenomenon. Even with efforts to control and stabilize GHGs, global temperatures are expected to rise by 1.8°F by the end of the 21st century. This change is irreversible due to the already elevated GHG levels in the atmosphere. Therefore, adapting to the changing climate becomes an ecological necessity.

Features of Adaptive Measures

Adaptation measures, such as constructing dikes and bulkheads to protect coastal properties from rising sea levels, come with significant costs. Existing adaptive strategies globally include climate-proof buildings and investments in drought-resistant systems to secure water and food during disasters.

Adaptation in Developing Countries

Developed nations, as major GHG emitters, have better adaptation capabilities. In contrast, developing nations, with lower emissions, often lack funds for adaptation strategies. This imbalance leaves them vulnerable to climate-related disasters like heatwaves, floods, and hurricanes. Funds have been set up to aid Least Developed Countries (LDCs) in meeting urgent adaptation needs.

FUN FACT

One tonne of recycled paper can save up to 20 barrels of oil, 7,000 gallons of water, 17 trees, and 4,200 kWh of electricity.

? Adaptation to climate change is a future necessity. (True/False)

Adaptation Measures

Individuals, communities, and organisations can contribute to climate change mitigation through various adaptation measures, including:

- Cultivating crops that are resilient to heat, drought, and waterlogging from heavy rainfall or flooding.
- Enhancing airflow in barns to provide shade for livestock during summer months.
- Enhancing evacuation routes in low-lying areas to safeguard residents during floods and sea storms.
- Preserving and enhancing migration corridors for animals to ensure safe migration.
- Increasing tree planting and creating green spaces in urban areas to mitigate heat.

Glossary

Abrupt: sudden

Adversely: unfavourably

Aerosol: a cloud of solid or liquid particles in a gas

Barren: having little or no vegetation; desolate and lifeless

Biodiversity: the diversity of plant and animal life in a particular habitat

Bulkhead: a partition that divides a ship or aircraft into compartments

Commence: cause to start

Dike: a barrier constructed to contain the flow of water or to keep out the sea

Disruption: disturbance that causes disorder

Diversity: the variety of things

Drastic: extreme effect

Ecosystem: refers to a community of organisms, their interaction with each other and their physical environment

Famine: a severe shortage of food resulting in violent hunger, starvation and death

Hibernation: a state of deep sleep in which an animal's heart rate and breathing slows down

Infectious: something that spreads easily

Irreversible: permanent

Kiloannum: the unit of time equal to one thousand years

Latitudinal: of or relating to latitudes north or south

Meteorologist: the one who studies the earth's atmosphere, weather and conditions

Ph scale: provides a measure on a scale from 0 to 14 of the acidity or alkalinity of a solution

Pollination: the transfer of pollen from the anther to the stigma of a plant

Potable: suitable for drinking

Precession: the wobbling motion of a spinning body (as a top) so that the axis of rotation sweeps out a cone

Precipitation: the water that falls on the ground in the form of rain, snow, hail, sleet or mist

Protocol: the original copy of any official document, for example, an agreement

Rainforest: a forest with heavy annual rainfall

Runoff: the occurrence of surplus liquid (as water)

Scarcity: the lack or shortage of something

Sustenance: the nourishment to sustain one's body

Symbiotic: the interaction between organisms (especially of different species) that live together and happen to benefit from each other

Troposphere: the lowest atmospheric layer; from 6 to 9 km high

Answers

Page 7 - Holocene Period
Page 8 - False
Page 9 - Chlorofluorocarbons
Page 10 - Axis
Page 11 - El Niño Southern Oscillation
Page 12 - False
Page 13 - True
Page 14 - Yes
Page 15 - True
Page 16 - False
Page 17 - Zooxanthellae
Page 18 - Boreal forests
Page 19 - Sea
Page 20 - About 1.2%
Page 21 - Yes
Page 22 - United Nations Framework Convention on Climate Change
Page 23 - Intergovernmental Panel on Climate Change
Page 24 - True

GLOBAL WARMING AND BIODIVERSITY

Introduction

Global warming poses a significant threat to biodiversity, which encompasses the entirety of living organisms on Earth, including their species and habitats.

As the planet undergoes warming, plants and animals attempt to adapt to the changing environments. However, the rapid pace of climate change presents challenges that some species struggle to overcome, rendering them vulnerable to extinction. Beyond rising temperatures, alterations in rainfall patterns, breeding seasons, and diminished interactions between animals and plants contribute to the endangerment of many species.

Scientists have predicted that if global temperatures increase by more than 3.5°C, up to 70 percent of the world's known species could face extinction.

It's Warming Up!

Global warming is causing the Earth's temperatures to rise, leading to various adverse effects such as altered precipitation patterns, melting polar ice, rising sea levels, and the depletion of rivers and lakes. Additionally, this phenomenon is pushing certain species to the brink of extinction.

The Arctic and Antarctica

The Arctic and Antarctica, typically covered with ice year-round, are experiencing significant ice melt due to rising temperatures. In 2002, a section of ice in Antarctica collapsed into the sea, equivalent in size to the state of Rhode Island. Scientists attribute this event to the weakening of the ice shelf by warm winds.

Lakes

Global warming has led to the drying up of many lakes worldwide. For instance, Lake Cachet in Chile vanished entirely, leaving only a large puddle in 2008. Additionally, the water levels of Lake Superior, the largest freshwater reservoir globally, have significantly decreased.

Rivers

The Ganges River in India, fed by the Gangotri Glacier, is beginning to run dry as the glacier shrinks. It is receding at an accelerated rate of 40 yards per year, nearly double the rate from 20 years ago. Many scientists predict that the glacier will vanish by 2030.

FUN FACT

Beneath the massive ice sheets of Antarctica and Greenland, there exist unique ecosystems of microbes and small invertebrates. These organisms thrive in extreme conditions, utilizing chemical energy from rocks and sediments.

? Where is Lake Cachet? ____________________

Changing Oceans and Seas

Global warming is altering the composition of oceans and seas, impacting the organisms that inhabit them. Plankton, including zooplankton and phytoplankton, as well as seagrass and kelp forests, are particularly vulnerable to rising water temperatures and increased carbon dioxide levels.

Phytoplankton

Phytoplankton, essential for many organisms, are small, plant-like organisms that float in water and produce their own food through photosynthesis. Their growth is influenced by water temperature, with faster growth in colder waters. If the oceans warm up, slowing phytoplankton growth, it could lead to reduced food availability for marine animals like fish, marine birds, and mammals.

Kelp Forests

Kelps, large seaweeds, form dense forests that serve as crucial habitats for marine life. They offer shelter and food to a diverse range of species including fish, lobsters, sea otters, seals, sea urchins, and jellyfish. However, these forests are increasingly threatened by rising sea temperatures, which are detrimental to the survival of kelp as they thrive in colder waters.

Seagrass

Seagrass is a flowering plant that grows entirely submerged in coastal waters, providing vital nursery grounds for various marine species. Rising sea levels and increasing carbon dioxide levels endanger seagrass, which in turn threatens the food sources and habitats of organisms like sea turtles, manatees, dugongs, seabirds, and sea urchins.

FUN FACT

Rising temperatures have increased the number of "dead zones," areas in oceans and seas with very low oxygen levels that cannot support life.

? Is seagrass a flowering plant or a non-flowering plant? ________

Struggling Life in the Oceans-I

Global warming is altering the distribution, abundance, and variety of marine life. Rising temperatures and increased absorption of carbon dioxide by oceans and seas are making marine waters more acidic. This acidification poses a serious threat to marine species and their survival.

Coral Reefs

Coral reefs, inhabited by over 25 percent of marine life, are formed by coral polyps. Rising sea temperatures negatively impact coral reefs by affecting the growth of algae, crucial for their survival. In warmer conditions with lower oxygen levels, corals expel algae, resulting in coral bleaching, ultimately leading to their death.

Fish

Rising temperatures and oxygen deficiency are disrupting fish life cycles. Some species reproduce early, while others face delays. Changes are seen in egg hatching times, growth rates, and spawning seasons. Climate change affects the metabolism of fish like Pacific salmon, requiring more food in warmer waters.

FUN FACT

Scientific studies have predicted that the, Great Barrier Reef could lose up to 95% of its corals by 2050 because of global warming.

Sea Turtles

Warmer temperatures could reduce the number of male sea turtle offspring, posing a threat to their population. The sex of sea turtle hatchlings is determined by the temperature of the water. Higher temperatures may decrease sea turtle births.

? Corals are formed by tiny organisms called ________.

Struggling Life in the Oceans-II

Since the start of the industrial revolution, ocean acidity has risen by 30 percent. This acidification has inflicted irreversible harm on marine life, and experts predict that its effects will intensify. If CO2 emissions persist at the current pace, certain sea species could face extinction by 2050.

Marine Calcifiers

Marine calcifiers, including mollusks, corals, and crustaceans, rely on calcium carbonate to form their shells. However, rising carbon dioxide levels in the water impede their ability to create new shells. The increasing acidity of oceans and seas poses a threat to these organisms, as their shells may begin to dissolve.

Whales

The declining population of plankton poses a threat to animals that rely on them for food. Whales are particularly affected, experiencing higher mortality rates and decreased reproduction due to insufficient nutrition. Killer whales, for example, have been observed feeding on sea otters, indicating shifts in their feeding habits likely caused by changing temperatures.

Lobsters

Rising temperatures compel cold-blooded creatures like lobsters to expend more energy on life processes such as respiration, growth, and reproduction. In the Gulf of Maine, warmer waters have extended the lobster growing season, leading to accelerated growth and earlier hatching. This benefits lobster populations but has adverse effects on species like cod, which feed on lobsters and have seen their numbers decline due to global warming.

? Is coral a marine calcifier?

____

FUN FACT

By 2100, it's projected that 60% of marine species may need to shift their habitats to remain within their preferred temperature ranges.

Melting Poles

Polar bears, seals, walruses, and penguins are the iconic animals of the polar regions. However, the melting sea ice presents significant challenges for these creatures. Adapted to extreme cold conditions, they rely on sea ice as a habitat and hunt other polar animals like Antarctic cod, dragonfish, and ice fish for food.

Seals

Rising temperatures are causing the premature melting of snow lairs that seals create to protect their pups from predators. Additionally, warming oceans in the Southern Ocean and the Arctic are melting sea ice, leading to a decline in fish and krill populations, vital food sources for seals.

Penguins

Penguins, flightless seabirds native to the Antarctic, rely on sea ice and extreme cold temperatures for breeding and rearing their chicks. Emperor penguins, for example, raise their offspring on the frozen sea for about seven months. However, disappearing sea ice threatens their habitats. Late formation and early retreat of sea ice, coupled with its overall shrinkage, pose significant challenges for penguins, potentially endangering their ability to rear their young.

? What is a penguin? ____________

Polar Bears

Polar bears, the largest carnivorous land animals, can reach heights of up to 3 metres and weigh up to 771 kilograms. They primarily hunt seals by breaking through sea ice where seals surface to breathe. However, with melting polar ice reducing their hunting grounds and shorter periods of sea ice coverage, polar bears face challenges in finding food.

FUN FACT

Continued sea ice loss is expected to lead to further range contraction for polar bears, with some populations facing localized extinctions.

Polar Life

Even slight changes in atmospheric temperatures in the polar regions impact a diverse array of life forms, including seabirds, plants, and the Inuit people. While some organisms can adapt to these changes, others struggle to do so.

Seabirds

Seabirds in the Arctic, including Arctic terns, Arctic skuas, and kittiwakes, are facing food shortages due to declining sand eel populations. This has resulted in significantly reduced chick production, with around 7,000 pairs of great skuas in the Shetlands producing only a few chicks. Starving adult birds have resorted to preying on their own offspring.

The Inuits

The Inuits, indigenous to the Arctic, rely heavily on polar bears for food and clothing. However, as polar bear populations decline due to warmer temperatures, the Inuits face food scarcity and a shortage of animal skin for clothing. Reduced hunting days, thinner sea ice, and thawing permafrost increase their exposure to danger. Moreover, the diminished snow and ice make it challenging for them to construct traditional igloos.

Polar Plants

Mosses and lichens, adapted to freezing temperatures, are common in polar regions. Additionally, Antarctic hairgrass and Antarctic pearlwort, native flowering plants, are flourishing in Antarctica as temperatures rise, expanding into areas once covered by ice sheets.

FUN FACT

Mosses and lichens survive during extreme winters by dehydrating and producing anti-freezing chemicals.

? Name two native flowering plants of Antarctica.

1. ________________ 2. ________________

Plants in Danger

Rising temperatures increase the risk of significant shifts in precipitation patterns, forest fires, droughts, and floods. Some regions experience heavier rainfall than usual, while others face delayed rains. Additionally, the timing of bud burst, leaf fall, pollination, and growth processes in trees and plants has changed.

Plants Cool the Earth

Plants and trees play a crucial role in the ecosystem by absorbing carbon dioxide and releasing oxygen, essential for all living organisms. They also contribute to cooling the atmosphere by releasing water vapor through pores on their leaves. However, increased carbon dioxide levels can lead to reduced water release from these pores, resulting in warmer temperatures in the surrounding environment.

Heat waves and Frost Days

Global warming prolongs heat waves and frost days, impacting various plant species. Extended warm summers also contribute to the proliferation of insects like the spruce bark beetle, which has devastated millions of spruce trees in Alaska.

FUN FACT

As CO2 levels rise, scientists anticipate faster growth and increased toxicity in plants like poison ivy, known to cause itchy rashes upon contact.

Droughts

Droughts are now affecting regions previously untouched by such conditions, depriving many plants of vital water and nutrients. Quiver trees in the Namib Desert are dwindling and vanishing from their natural habitat due to these extended dry spells.

Quiver trees

? Poison ivy cannot grow in CO2 rich environments. (True or False)

Forests at Risk

Forests, covering one-third of the Earth's surface, are vital ecosystems supporting diverse wildlife. Minor shifts in temperature and precipitation can have significant impacts on both forests and their inhabitants. The heightened risk of forest fires has seen a notable increase in wildfires in recent years.

Trees on the Move

Increasing temperatures are driving many organisms to migrate towards cooler areas. This shift is evident in plants and trees moving towards the poles. Species like American basswood, northern white cedar, black ash, sugar maple, yellow birch, and bigtooth aspen are all heading northward. Notably, basswood and maple have moved nearly 50 km in response to these changes.

Conserve Forests

Forests store up to 80 percent of the carbon on land. If deforestation continues, about 1.7 billion tons of carbon could be released into the atmosphere annually. Rainforests, such as the Amazon, are significant reservoirs of carbon dioxide and play a crucial role in mitigating global warming. However, rising carbon dioxide levels are affecting plant growth in the Amazon, leading to slow growth and rapid die-off of many trees.

Changing Tree Lines

Climatic conditions determine the tree line—the natural limit to where trees can grow—and changes in this line can impact a region's climate. As temperatures rise, tree lines are shifting farther north to areas where the climate is more suitable for growth. This movement brings a greater diversity of wildlife, disrupting native ecosystems and potentially causing imbalance.

FUN FACT

Almost half of the Alpine plants on Mt Kosciuszko in Australia are threatened because of global warming.

? Forests store ________ of the carbon present on land.

Threat to Wildlife

Global warming poses the most significant threat to Earth's wildlife. The rapid climate change often outpaces the ability of many species to adapt, breed, or migrate to more suitable habitats. Additionally, changes in climatic patterns affect their food sources. Studies suggest that as much as 37 percent of all plant and animal species could face extinction by 2050 due to climate change.

Lemurs

Changes in temperature and rainfall patterns can impact the reproductive capabilities of female lemurs. Lemurs are less active during heavy rains, reducing the likelihood of successful births. Furthermore, heavy rains lead to fruit falling off trees, affecting food availability for baby lemurs. This scarcity of food can make it challenging for infants to survive. The Milne-Edward's sifaka lemur, found in Madagascar, is among the species threatened by global warming.

Primates

Plants in warmer climates have leaves with higher fibre and less digestible protein, slowing down digestion for leaf-eating animals. Elevated temperatures also force some gorillas and monkeys to seek shade during the day, affecting their foraging, social interactions, and territory defence. This reduced activity, combined with less nutritious food, poses a threat to mountain gorillas and colobus monkeys, potentially leading to extinction.

Koala

Koalas, which only feed on eucalyptus leaves, are affected by the changing nutrient balance in these trees due to increased atmospheric carbon dioxide. This alters the nutritional quality of the leaves, rendering them less suitable for koalas' survival. As a consequence, koalas are at risk of extinction due to malnutrition and starvation.

FUN FACT

Soay sheep on the Scottish island of Hirta have shrunk by 5% on average since 1985. Scientists blame the shrinking on climate change, specifically milder winters.

? Koalas feed on eucalyptus tree leaves. (True or False)

Amphibians Facing Peril

Amphibians, such as frogs and toads, are particularly vulnerable to even minor fluctuations in temperature due to their unique dual habitat lifestyle, which makes them excellent indicators of environmental change.

Unsafe Amphibians

Amphibians have thin, moist skin protected by a layer of mucus, requiring them to remain near water to prevent dehydration. Their sensitivity to slight variations in temperature, humidity, and air and water quality makes them highly susceptible to environmental changes.

Effects on Amphibians

Rising temperatures facilitate the proliferation of bacteria and fungi, leading to disease outbreaks among amphibians. Research indicates a weakening immune system in amphibians, resulting in life-threatening illnesses and population declines. With fewer amphibians to regulate insect populations, the increase in insects poses a potential threat.

Breeding

The breeding season of amphibians hinges on environmental temperature and moisture levels. They lay vulnerable, jelly-like eggs that require constant moisture to survive. Amphibians in temperate regions face significant threats from global warming, disrupting their hibernation patterns and prompting early breeding. Increased temperatures can trigger premature breeding, leaving them susceptible to weather extremes such as snowmelt floods and early winters.

FUN FACT

Amphibians are more vulnerable to climate change than other vertebrate groups, with about 43% of species threatened with extinction.

? Salamander is an amphibian. (True or False)

Reptiles in Trouble

Reptiles, such as lizards, crocodiles, snakes, turtles, and tortoises, are cold-blooded creatures with scaly skin. They are adjusting to climate change by changing where they live and how they behave, in response to global warming. As temperatures increase, reptiles may change their nesting, feeding, and activity patterns, causing shifts in their distribution and ecological interactions.

Effects on Reptiles

Reptiles are highly responsive to shifts in air and water quality, temperature, and rainfall, but they are more adaptable to warmer and drier conditions compared to amphibians. They regulate their body temperature by basking in the sun for warmth and seeking shade to cool down when temperatures rise. With increasing temperatures, reptiles are spending more time seeking shade, which impacts their foraging activities.

Breeding

Rising temperatures and changing rainfall patterns can alter the timing of breeding, egg laying, and hatching in reptiles. For example, lizards typically reproduce in spring, but high temperatures may disrupt their breeding cycles. Additionally, rising sea levels threaten the nesting grounds of marine reptiles like sea turtles, while increased air and water temperatures can impact their reproductive success.

Male or Female

The gender of baby reptiles is determined by the temperature during incubation. Warmer temperatures tend to result in the hatching of male reptiles, while colder temperatures favor the hatching of female reptiles.

FUN FACT

By 2080, 39% of local lizard populations and 20% of worldwide lizard species are predicted to go extinct due to climate change.

? What type of skin do reptiles have? ____________________

Insects Around the World

Insects, known for their remarkable biological diversity, play crucial roles in ecosystems worldwide. They exhibit a remarkable sensitivity to changes in temperature and habitat, earning them the designation of environmental indicators.

Insects Facing Climate Hazards

Temperature changes affect insect behaviour, distribution, life cycle, and reproduction. Due to their short lifespan and rapid reproductive rates, insects respond more swiftly to climate change than longer-lived organisms like plants and animals. Warmer temperatures facilitate increased reproduction among insects such as mosquitoes and beetles, posing adverse effects on humans and other living organisms.

Tropics and Temperate

In the tropics, where temperatures remain constant year-round, insects struggle to adapt to temperature fluctuations, potentially leading to species extinction. Conversely, in temperate regions, insects are adapting to changing temperatures, resulting in population increases.

Insects and Pollination

Pollination occurs when pollen from one flower is transferred to another by insects like bumblebees, butterflies, and flies. However, changes in early-season climate, such as warmer and drier conditions, are causing flowers to bloom earlier when pollinators may not be present. Consequently, plants struggle to reproduce, and when insects do arrive, there are fewer flowers available for them to feed on.

FUN FACT

By 2050, climate change is expected to drive approximately 15–37% of these species to extinction.

? What is the process of transferring pollens called? ____________

Impact on Butterflies

Butterflies are sensitive to temperature shifts. With the Earth warming and climate patterns altering, butterflies are relocating to areas with more favourable climates. Butterflies play a crucial role in pollination and are important indicators of ecosystem health, making their response to climate change a significant concern for biodiversity.

Effects on Butterflies

Butterflies are feeling the impact of climate change, particularly in lowland areas near sea level where their diversity is declining. Warmer temperatures and habitat loss due to human activities are driving this trend, forcing these species to migrate to higher, cooler altitudes. Conversely, high-elevation butterflies are also experiencing a decrease in diversity as they struggle to adapt to rising temperatures in colder regions.

Benefitting Butterflies

Some butterfly species are thriving in response to changing climate conditions. For instance, the Brown Argus butterfly has adapted by altering its diet, leading to a flourishing population in Britain over the past two decades. Similarly, the Comma butterfly is increasing in numbers and expanding its habitat northward. There are also predictions that the Swallowtail butterfly will extend its range further north, including into northwestern Europe.

Monarch Migrations

Global warming threatens the population of Monarch butterflies, famous for their migratory journey from Canada and the US to Mexico. Climate change alters their habitat with wetter, colder winters and drier, hotter summers disrupting their migration and hibernation patterns.

FUN FACT

The Monarch butterfly is also referred to as Milkweed butterfly and Wanderer butterfly.

? The monarch butterfly is also known as __________.

Impact on Birds-I

Increasing temperatures threaten birds' habitats and food sources. Seasonal changes prompt birds to respond to early spring weather, potentially causing them to migrate north prematurely, where food may be scarce due to lingering snow.

Changing Behaviour

Rising temperatures are altering bird behaviours. For instance, Rocky Mountain Robins are laying eggs about two weeks earlier in spring than in previous years, but food sources for their hatchlings aren't available yet. Similarly, many bird species in Britain have shifted to earlier egg-laying patterns.

Tropical Birds

Birds in the tropics face heightened vulnerability to climate change. Droughts and irregular dry seasons are diminishing their populations, particularly those that breed during the wet season when food is abundant. For example, toucans in the Costa Rican lowlands are relocating to higher-altitude cloud forests, where they compete with native birds like quetzals for nest space and prey on their eggs and nestlings.

A toucan

? Is toucan a tropical bird?

____

What will happen?

As temperatures rise, birds like the North American warbler and golden-winged warbler are migrating northward for cooler climates. Species unable to adapt their habitat, such as the red-cockaded woodpecker in the southeastern US, face a higher risk of extinction.

FUN FACT

According to studies, more that 80 percent birds spend at least some time in the tropics.

Impact on Birds-II

Rising temperatures are disrupting the natural cycles of animals and birds. Migration timings, destinations, and reproductive routines of birds are shifting in response to climate change. For example, higher spring temperatures are drying up breeding habitats of birds like waterfowl.

Blue-winged teals

Birds are Shrinking

A study by the Australian National University revealed that birds in southeastern Australia have shrunk by 2-4 percent compared to their historical size. This change has been attributed to climate change, as average daily temperatures in Australia have risen by 0.7 degrees Celsius over the same period. The study suggests that smaller bodies help birds shed heat more efficiently in warmer temperatures.

Facing Potential Extinction

Birds are adapting to changing climates by altering their habitats, but those unable to adjust nesting locations face extinction risks. Passerine species like the variegated fairy-wren and yellow-rumped thornbill are particularly threatened. Additionally, tawny eagle populations in Africa and Asia are declining due to shifting rainfall patterns.

A fairy-wren

A tawny eagle

Waterfowls

Global warming is altering waterfowl habitats and breeding patterns in North America's Prairie Pothole Region, a critical breeding area. Prolonged dry seasons and drought are drying up the region, negatively impacting breeding for duck species like mallards, blue-winged teal, gadwall, canvasbacks, ruddy ducks, and northern pintails, causing population declines.

A gadwall

FUN FACT

A study has found that 66–73% of 1,091 bird species may move north or higher by 2070 due to climate change.

? Birds are shrinking in size due to global warming. (True or False)

Impact on Migration

Global changes in temperature, precipitation, and seasonal length are disrupting migration patterns and timings for animals worldwide. This interference poses challenges for animals seeking to avoid harsh weather conditions, find food, or breed, prompting alterations in their traditional migratory routes and behaviours.

Threat to Migrating Animals

Rising temperatures, early springs, prolonged dry summers, and short, harsh winters pose challenges for many migrating animals, affecting their ability to accurately time their journeys. Delaying departure risks insufficient food reserves, while arriving early at their destination may lead to competition with resident species for resources.

Siberian Crane

The Siberian Crane, a migratory bird, inhabits the Arctic tundra of western and eastern Russia. With only around 3,000 remaining, they face extinction as their habitat diminishes due to global warming. During winter, the eastern population migrates to China, while the western population heads to Iran. However, reduced precipitation and heavy rainfall in China pose additional threats to their survival.

Storm Petrel

Storm petrels migrate from the North Atlantic breeding grounds to Namibia, South Africa, and the Indian Ocean. Their ability to store fat reserves for the journey depends on climate and migration routes, both of which are affected by global warming.

FUN FACT

Bar-tailed godwits make a nonstop flight, covering a distance of 11,000 km in eight days.

?

Animals that move from one place to another seasonally or for reproduction are called _______.

Impact on Hibernation

Hibernation is a natural state of deep sleep that many animals, including ground squirrels, bears, and chipmunks, enter to endure harsh cold temperatures. Typically, these animals rely on temperature cues to initiate and end hibernation. However, the phenomenon of global warming is disrupting this natural cycle.

Marmots

Marmots, large ground squirrels inhabiting mountainous regions of Europe and Asia, hibernate for eight months to endure long winters, awakening when the climate warms. This extended growing season boosts their breeding and growth. However, with global warming, marmots are waking from hibernation approximately 38 days earlier than normal.

American Robin

American Robins migrate to lower mountains for winter and return to breed in higher elevations in Colorado during summer. They are now arriving 14 days earlier, but this means they must wait longer for snow to melt before finding food and nesting.

Brown Bears

Global warming threatens brown bears as warmer winters disrupt their hibernation patterns. In Spain's northern Cantabrian Mountains, European brown bears are observed to forgo hibernation entirely, leading to increased aggression and stress.

Threat

Many animals hibernate to evade harsh cold conditions that impede their ability to forage for food. Throughout hibernation, they rely on stored energy reserves as their heart rate and metabolic processes slow down. When they emerge from hibernation, they require ample food intake. However, climate change disrupts the availability of food sources during this critical period, leading to starvation among these animals.

FUN FACT

Lemmings hibernate in burrows beneath the snow, but unexpected rainfall can lead to the formation of ice over their burrows, making it difficult for them to emerge.

? What are marmots?

____

Climate Change Affects All

Global warming impacts humans as profoundly as it does other living organisms. Elevated temperatures contribute to the drying up of lakes and rivers, resulting in water scarcity. Erratic rainfall patterns adversely affect agricultural yields, consequently leading to food shortages.

Invasive Species

Some species are adapting to climate change by migrating to new habitats, expanding their range, and becoming invasive species. For example, the horse chestnut leaf miner, a moth, has migrated to European countryside due to warmer climates, damaging chestnut trees by feeding on their leaves. Similarly, the Colorado beetle has spread to Europe and Russia, causing significant destruction to potato crops.

A Colorado beetle

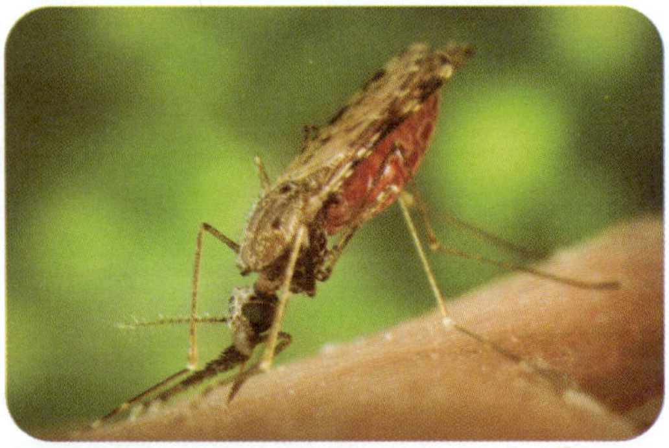
An anopheles mosquito feeding on a human host. Anopheles mosquitoes are responsible for causing malaria.

Threat to Humans

Deaths attributed to changes in temperature, humidity, rainfall, snowfall patterns, and smog are increasing. Higher temperatures also promote the breeding of disease-carrying insects like mosquitoes, spreading diseases like malaria and dengue fever beyond tropical regions. The World Health Organisation (WHO) reports that 150,000 people die annually due to climate change-related issues.

FUN FACT

The rise in smog levels over the next two decades could lead to an 80% increase in deaths related to smog.

? What does the WHO stand for? ____________________

Glossary

Atmosphere: the blanket of gases enveloping the earth.

Budburst: the growing of new leaves at the beginning of each growing season.

Calcium carbonate: a white solid compound found in chalk, limestone, and in animal shells and bones.

Climate: the weather conditions of a particular place.

Cue: a clue or signal.

Dengue fever: a virus-caused disease spread by mosquitoes, involving high fever, rashes on the body, headache, and vomiting.

Disrupt: to interrupt or stop something.

Endangered: an organism that is facing danger and is about to go extinct.

Environment: the surroundings or conditions in which a person, animal, or plant lives.

Extinct: to no longer exist.

Forage: to search for food.

Habitat: the natural home or environment of a living organism.

Immune system: the body's defense system that fights with germs to prevent infections and diseases.

Incubation: a process to keep eggs warm until the time babies develop and come out.

Krill: a very small shrimp-like crustacean.

Lichen: a very small, soft, and slow-growing plant.

Malaria: a mosquito-borne disease of humans that involves fevers, chills, and flu-like symptoms.

Malnutrition: a medical condition in which a person does not get enough nutrients in his/her diet.

Metabolism: a process by which food is converted into energy.

Mortality rate: the measurement of the number of deaths against the population of an area.

Moss: soft green or brown plant that grows in layers on wet ground, rocks, or trees.

Passerine: related to birds known for having feet most suitable for perching on trees.

Permafrost: ground that remains permanently frozen all year round.

Plankton: very tiny organisms that include both zooplankton and phytoplankton.

Precipitation: water that falls to the ground in the form of either rain, snow, hail, or sleet.

Sand eel: a snake-like marine fish.

Spawn: the release or deposition of eggs by a fish, frog, mollusk, etc.

Symbiotic relationship: a relationship between two living organisms in which both benefit each other.

Thaw: when ice or snow turns liquid due to high temperature.

Tundra: the arctic region of europe, asia, and north america.

Voyage: a long journey.

Vulnerable: someone or something that can be easily harmed or attacked.

Waterfowl: birds that spend most of their life in or near water.

Answers

Page 29 - Chile, South America
Page 30 - Flowering plant
Page 31 - Coral Polyps
Page 32 - Yes
Page 33 - A flightless seabird
Page 34 - Antarctic hairgrass and Antarctic pearlwort
Page 35 - False
Page 36 - 80 percent
Page 37 - True
Page 38 - False
Page 39 - Scaly skin
Page 40 - Pollination
Page 41 - Wanderer butterfly
Page 42 - Yes
Page 43 - True
Page 44 - Migratory animals
Page 45 - Large ground squirrel
Page 46 - World Health Organization

GREENHOUSE GASES AND THE OZONE LAYER

Introduction

The Earth's atmosphere, composed of various gases, includes greenhouse gases (GHGs) capable of trapping heat radiated by the Earth, maintaining a slightly warmer climate through the greenhouse effect, vital for sustaining life. However, human activities disrupt this balance by releasing excessive GHGs, harming global climate and topography.

Global warming, caused by increased GHGs, raises sea levels and warms the atmosphere. Daily human activities add GHGs like CO_2, methane, and nitrous oxide to the atmosphere, underscoring the urgent need for individuals and businesses to reduce their carbon footprint to combat global warming.

Greenhouse Effect

An increase in GHG concentration amplifies the greenhouse effect, elevating Earth's surface temperature and causing global warming, thereby driving significant climatic changes on our planet.

Heating the Atmosphere

About 31 percent of solar radiation is reflected back into space, while the Earth's atmosphere absorbs the remaining 69 percent. Sunlight passing through the atmosphere heats the Earth's surface, causing it to emit infrared rays that warm the air above. Greenhouse gases in the atmosphere absorb and re-emit this infrared radiation, acting like a greenhouse glass, which traps heat and prevents it from escaping.

The greenhouse effect

Human Contribution

Human activities, like excessive burning of fossil fuels, release additional GHGs into the atmosphere, heightening the greenhouse effect. While CO_2, methane, and nitrous oxide are the main contributors, other gases also play a role, albeit in smaller quantities.

? What percentage of the sun's radiation is reflected back into space? ____________

FUN FACT

The concentration of CO_2 was less during the glacial periods. Such periods were marked by colder temperatures.

Greenhouse Gases

GHGs in our atmosphere have facilitated life on Earth by trapping solar heat, which maintains a warmer and more stable temperature. Common GHGs include methane, CO_2, nitrogen oxides (NOx), and fluorinated gases (F-gases). Acting like a blanket, GHGs keep Earth's temperature approximately 30 degrees warmer than it would be otherwise.

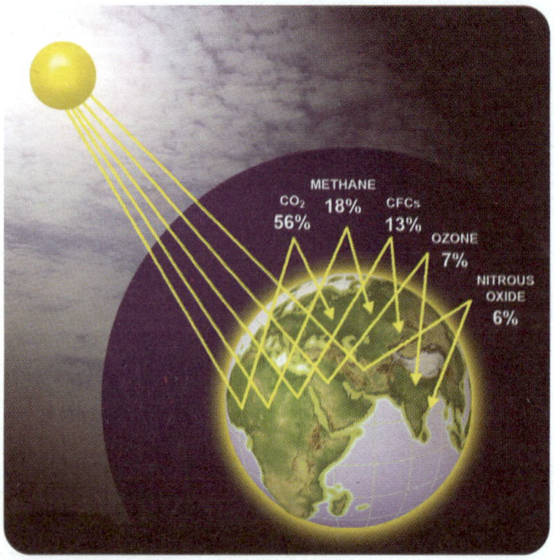

Constitution of GHGs in the atmosphere

Constitution

GHGs make up only 1 percent of the total atmosphere, with oxygen and nitrogen comprising the rest. While some GHGs like water vapour occur naturally, others like chlorofluorocarbons are released due to human activities. Different GHGs have varying durations in the atmosphere and warming capabilities.

How GHGs work?

GHGs permit sunlight to enter the atmosphere unhindered. Once sunlight reaches the Earth's surface, a portion is reflected back into space as infrared radiation. GHGs absorb this infrared radiation, trapping its heat within the atmosphere. Comprised of three or more atoms loosely bonded, GHG molecules absorb and vibrate with heat, releasing it thereafter to be absorbed by other molecules. This process facilitates the trapping and transfer of heat by GHGs.

Global Warming Potential (GWP)

GWP, or Global Warming Potential, is a measure that estimates a gas's contribution to global warming relative to CO_2. It is determined by the ratio of heat trapped by one unit mass of the greenhouse gas to that of one unit mass of CO_2.

FUN FACT

CO_2 stays in the atmosphere for up to 1,000 years, methane for around a decade, and nitrous oxide for approximately 120 years.

? GHGs keep the earth's temperature ______ warmer.

Methane

Methane (CH4) is an odourless and colourless gas that significantly contributes to the greenhouse effect. It is the simplest hydrocarbon and highly combustible. Methane is responsible for almost half of the planet's human-induced warming.

Uses

Methane has a GWP of 21, making it 21 times more effective than CO_2 in trapping heat. Its direct release into the atmosphere contributes to global warming. To mitigate environmental issues, methane is utilised as a fuel for energy generation.

Sources

Methane is naturally generated through the decomposition of organic matter in oxygen-deprived environments such as wetlands, rice paddies, termites, oceans, permafrost, and wildfires. Human activities such as managing landfills, addressing natural gas leaks, agricultural practices, fossil fuel extraction, wastewater treatment, and specific industrial processes, also contribute significantly to global methane emissions, accounting for 75%.

Cattle

Ruminant animals possess four stomachs and a distinctive digestive system. They emit methane during digestion as they graze on plant matter. A cow typically produces 80-110 kilograms of methane annually. Globally, ruminant animals release approximately 80 million metric tonnes of methane annually.

FUN FACT

Methane produces more heat and light energy than other fossil fuels, while producing less carbon dioxide and other pollutants.

? How much methane is released in the atmosphere by ruminants annually?

Carbon Dioxide

CO_2 is an atmospheric gas composed of one carbon atom and two oxygen atoms in each molecule. It is generated through the combustion of carbon compounds and through respiration. CO_2 is a greenhouse gas and plays a significant role in global warming. Once emitted, it can persist in the atmosphere for up to 100 years.

Increase in CO_2

The atmospheric concentration of CO_2 has risen by approximately 30 percent since the early 1800s. Human activities, including the burning of fossil fuels and deforestation, have significantly contributed to this increase. CO_2 is directly produced through the combustion of organic matter in the presence of oxygen.

Human Activities

Since the Industrial Revolution, atmospheric concentrations of CO_2 have increased by up to 36 percent by 2006. The use of fossil fuels in vehicles, power plants, and industries releases significant amounts of CO_2. Deforestation further exacerbates this issue by hindering the accumulation of carbon in plants. To mitigate climate change, it is essential to focus on energy efficiency and reduce energy consumption.

Volcanic eruptions release large amounts of CO_2 into the atmosphere

Natural Sources and Sinks

All animals, including humans, exhale CO_2 as part of the respiration process. Plants absorb CO_2 for nutrition and growth and emit oxygen in return. Various microorganisms produce CO_2 through fermentation. Volcanic eruptions and hot springs also emit CO_2. Oceans serve as a significant carbon sink, absorbing large quantities of CO_2 from the sea surfaces.

FUN FACT

CO_2 in its dry form is known as dry ice.

? Plants absorb CO_2 and release ____________.

Water Vapour

Water vapour is the gaseous form of water in our atmosphere, representing the most abundant and important greenhouse gas. Water transitions into vapour through processes such as evaporation, sublimation, and transpiration. Clouds, fog, and haze are various manifestations of water vapour.

Sources and Sinks

Water vapour has a short atmospheric lifetime, continually replenished through evaporation and removed via condensation as rain and snow. Atmospheric water vapour is reactive and challenging to measure due to fluctuating weather conditions. Its concentrations vary between locations, with higher temperatures typically resulting in increased water vapour levels.

Effects

Water vapour accounts for approximately 95 percent of global warming. As the Earth's average temperature rises, so does the average evaporation rate. Warmer air has a greater capacity to hold moisture, leading to higher concentrations of water vapour in the atmosphere, which in turn absorb more heat. Consequently, the increase in water vapour intensifies the greenhouse effect and global warming, creating a vicious circle.

Clouds

Increased water vapour in the atmosphere, caused by global warming, results in more cloud formation. These additional clouds contribute to trapping more heat within the atmosphere. However, clouds also play a moderating role in climate by reflecting a portion of solar radiation. Low, thick clouds reflect radiation and cool the Earth's surface, while high, thin clouds trap heat and warm the surface.

FUN FACT

Boiling water produces steam, which comprises up to 70 percent of the total greenhouse effect.

? Warmer air holds more water vapour. (True or false)

Nitrous Oxide

Nitrous oxide (N_2O) is a colourless greenhouse gas with a sweet odour, boasting a high GWP of 310 and a long lifetime. It is also capable of depleting ozone. Known as 'laughing gas', it induces tingling sensations and euphoria upon consumption, making it useful as a sedative in the medical field.

Denitrification

N_2O is naturally produced through the breakdown of nitrogen by bacteria in soils and oceans, a process known as denitrification. Nutrient-rich discharges into the world's oceans, such as agricultural run-off and sewage, have led to significant denitrification in open water. These biological processes account for over 60 percent of N_2O production.

Sinks

The majority of atmospheric N_2O is removed from the stratosphere through reaction with light and excited oxygen atoms, a process known as photolysis. Additionally, a small portion of N_2O is converted into nitrogen gas by bacteria in the soil.

Man-made Sources

Human-influenced sources of N_2O include animal manure management and the growing use of fertilizers in agriculture. Industrial activities such as combustion in fossil fuel-fired power plants, nylon production, nitric acid production, and vehicle emissions also contribute to the rise in N_2O levels. Concentrations of N_2O have increased since the onset of the industrial revolution.

FUN FACT

Nitrous Oxide works well for patients with mental or physical disabilities, or for those with a lower pain tolerance, as it can reduce the pain of certain dental procedures.

? What is the process of breaking down of nitrogen in soil called?

Other GHGs-I

Apart from the five major greenhouse gases in the atmosphere, trace quantities of other greenhouse gases include various fluorinated gases and halocarbons. These gases have lifetimes ranging from a few months to over 4,000 years, with global warming potentials (GWPs) up to 10,000 times that of CO_2. They are primarily used in various industrial processes.

Chlorofluorocarbons

Chlorofluorocarbons (CFCs) are compounds made up of carbon, chlorine, and fluorine. These toxic substances, with a faintly sweet odour, were formerly employed in aerosol applications, refrigerants, and solvents. Despite their prohibition, CFCs persist in the atmosphere, contributing to the greenhouse effect due to their extended atmospheric lifetimes.

Black Carbon

Black carbon, though not a greenhouse gas, ranks second to CO_2 in trapping atmospheric heat. Composed of tiny particles mixing with dust, sulphates, and other ground emissions, it rises through the atmosphere, mixing with clouds and water droplets before returning to Earth through precipitation. Settling on ice and snow, it darkens their reflective surfaces, exacerbating global warming. Soot from various sources like chimneys, stoves, fires, vehicles, ships, kilns, and flares accelerates this process.

Hydrofluorocarbons (HFCs)

HFCs, compounds of hydrogen, fluorine, and carbon, were adopted as alternatives to chlorofluorocarbons in refrigeration and air conditioning to mitigate ozone depletion. With lifetimes ranging from 14 to 260 years and high global warming potential, they present significant environmental concerns. To tackle global warming, it's essential to phase out HFCs from the atmosphere and ensure proper disposal of existing refrigerants.

FUN FACT

The most common HFC warms the planet 3,790 times more than carbon dioxide over 20 years.

? What is the atmospheric lifetime range of HFCs? ____________

Other GHGs-II

Other greenhouse gases with particularly significant impacts include fluorocarbons, sulphur hexafluoride, and nitrogen trifluoride. Despite their relatively low concentrations, these gases significantly contribute to global warming. They can persist in the atmosphere for hundreds to thousands of years.

Cosmetic products such as lipsticks may contain perfluorocarbons.

Sulphur Hexafluoride (SF_6)

Sulphur hexafluoride (SF6) is a colourless, odourless, nontoxic, and non-flammable man-made gas, considered the most potent greenhouse gas with a GWP exceeding 100 over a 100-year period. Its atmospheric lifetime can reach up to 3,200 years. SF6 experienced a 7 percent increase during the 1980s and 1990s and is mainly used in magnesium-producing industries.

Perfluorocarbons

Fluorocarbons or perfluorocarbons are potent greenhouse gases characterized by strong carbon and fluorine bonds, with atmospheric lifetimes exceeding 1000 years. These man-made chemicals, composed primarily of fluorine and carbon, are typically non-reactive, odourless, and colourless gases. They find application in diverse sectors, including medical applications, cosmetics, and semiconductor manufacturing.

FUN FACT

SF6 is the most potent greenhouse gas in existence with a global warming potential of 23,900 times the baseline of CO_2.

? NF3 has a GWP of ________ over a 100-year timescale.

Nitrogen Trifluoride (NF_3)

Nitrogen trifluoride (NF3) is a synthetic, colourless, and stable gas with a toxic odour. Used in the production of flat-screen TVs, computer screens, and cell phones, it has a high global warming potential (GWP) of 17,200 over a 100-year period and an atmospheric lifetime of 740 years. Recent research suggests NF3 concentrations are four times higher than expected.

The manufacturing process of flat screen TVs use NF_3.

Indirect GHGs

Some indirect greenhouse gases contribute to the greenhouse effect by forming substances that enhance it once released into the atmosphere. Examples include carbon monoxide (CO), hydrogen gas, non-methane volatile organic compounds, ammonia, and sulphur dioxide.

Automobiles emit high levels of carbon monoxide.

Carbon Monoxide (CO)

Carbon monoxide (CO) is a toxic gas resulting from incomplete fossil fuel combustion. It increases the global warming potential of greenhouse gases by depleting hydroxyl (OH) radicals, essential for breaking down gases like carbon dioxide and methane. Additionally, CO contributes to the formation of tropospheric ozone and carbon dioxide, major greenhouse gases. It is short-lived and prevalent in densely populated areas, primarily emitted by automobiles and charcoal burning.

Hydrogen Gas

Hydrogen gas, a potential future fuel replacement for fossil fuels, is utilized in various applications. However, inevitable leaks from cars, production sites, and transportation contribute to atmospheric hydrogen levels. Should hydrogen fully replace fossil fuels, annual atmospheric discharges could range from 60 to 120 trillion grams. Additionally, hydrogen production from natural gas and fossil fuel burning releases carbon dioxide.

FUN FACT

Hydrogen gas is lighter than air.

? Aldehydes are volatile organic compounds. (True or False)

Volatile Organic Compounds

Volatile organic compounds (VOCs) are weak indirect greenhouse gases aiding in tropospheric ozone formation. They comprise non-methane hydrocarbons, alcohols, aldehydes, and organic acids, mainly emitted by natural sources like plants and oceans. VOCs also result from petrol and diesel evaporation and incomplete biomass burning.

GHGs and Global Warming

Since 1920, Earth's surface temperature has increased by 1.4°F, with current warming happening much faster. From 1990 to 2007, CO_2 emissions from fossil fuels rose by 21.8%, while methane and nitrous oxide emissions saw slight declines. The increased CO_2 concentration has led to major climate changes.

Plant and Animal Life

Global warming has indeed had serious effects on plant and animal life. There are observable shifts, such as earlier blooming of flowers and earlier breeding among animals. Habitat loss, food scarcity, and rising temperatures have led to the extinction of many species. Ecosystems, including the Arctic region, are being destroyed, and food chains are disrupted due to climate and temperature changes.

Weather Changes

Global warming is indeed leading to an increase in floods, storms, and droughts. Elevated temperatures result in a higher rate of evaporation, leading to increased rainfall. The melting of polar ice caps, caused by global warming, has the potential to raise sea levels, thereby posing a risk of submergence for coastal and low-lying regions.

Agriculture and Forests

Warmer temperatures and greenhouse gas emissions are affecting agriculture. Irregular rainfall and drying of agricultural lands are leading causes of crop failures. Global temperature rise has also led to an increase in disease-causing microorganisms and pests, resulting in widespread crop diseases and reduced productivity.

Corn crops destroyed by untimely rains.

? CO_2 emissions have increased by ________ since 1990 to 2007.

FUN FACT

The hottest temperature ever recorded on Earth was 134°F (56.7°C) on July 10, 1913 at Greenland Ranch in Death Valley, California. Death Valley is a dry desert region that's 190 feet below sea level.

Ozone Layer

Ozone, a gas composed of three oxygen atoms, is blue in colour and possesses a strong odour. It forms a broad layer in the stratosphere, spanning from 15 to 30 kilometers above Earth's surface. Ozone is generated through the reaction of oxygen atoms with ultraviolet radiation.

Ozone Concentration

The ozone layer's thickness varies depending on latitude, sunspots, and seasons. Although the total ozone mass in the atmosphere is around three billion metric tonnes, it comprises only 0.00006 percent of the atmosphere. The highest ozone concentration is typically found at an altitude of approximately 32 kilometres above Earth's surface.

Protective Shield

The ozone layer shields life on Earth by blocking harmful UV rays from reaching the surface, earning it the nickname "Earth's sunscreen." It absorbs 97-99 percent of high-frequency UV radiation, which can cause diseases like skin cancer and cataracts. Elevated UV radiation levels can also reduce crop yields, disrupt the marine food chain, and cause other environmental issues.

Damage

Over 60 years, human activity has harmed the ozone layer through chemicals and pollution, resulting in its depletion, known as the ozone hole.

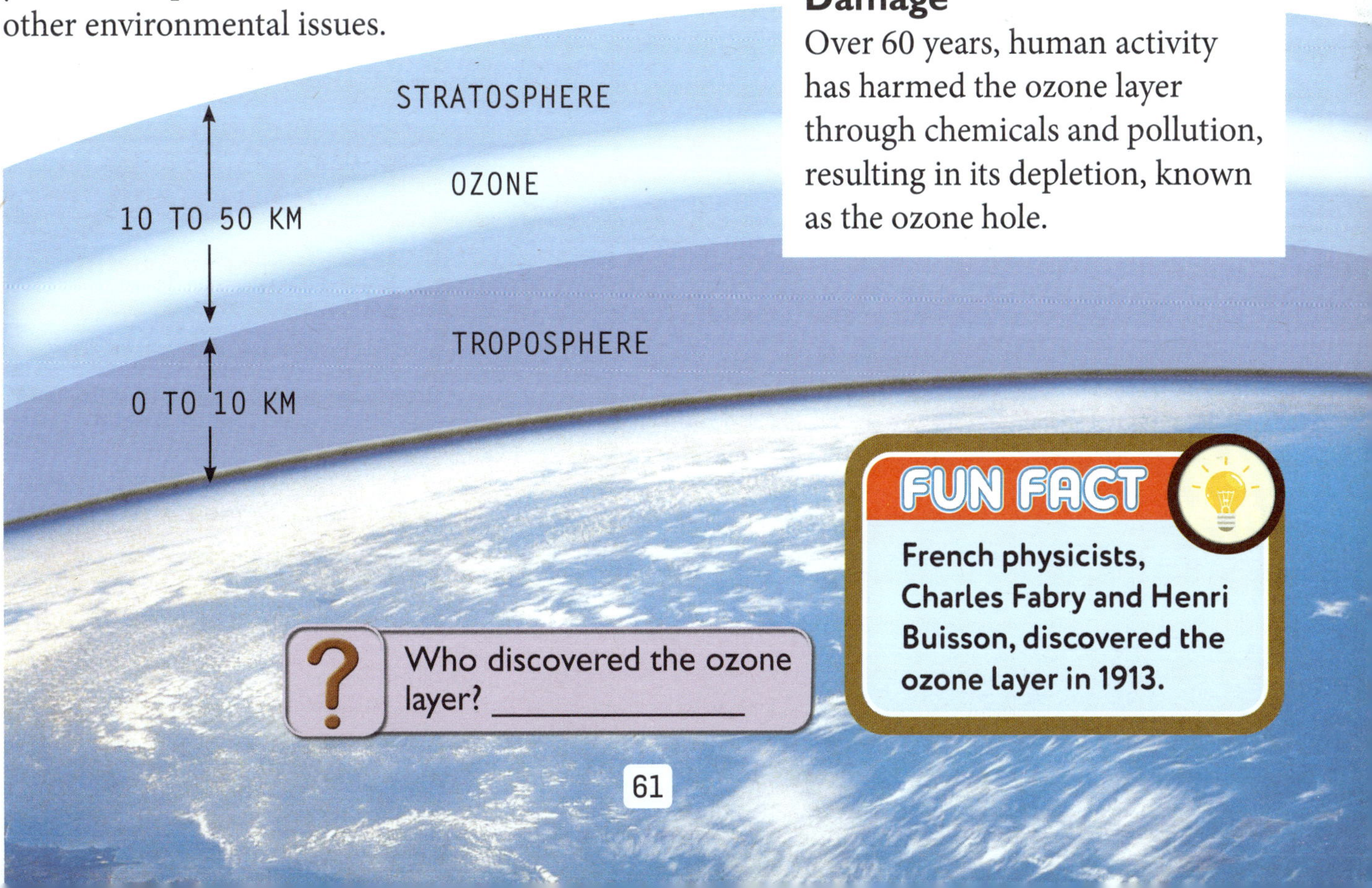

FUN FACT

French physicists, Charles Fabry and Henri Buisson, discovered the ozone layer in 1913.

? Who discovered the ozone layer? ______________

Tropospheric Ozone

Ozone is found in both the upper atmosphere (stratosphere) and near the ground (troposphere). While the stratospheric ozone layer protects life on Earth, ground-level ozone is a pollutant causing health and environmental problems. Additionally, it acts as a greenhouse gas, contributing to global warming.

GWP of Ozone

Ozone is about 3,000 times more potent than CO_2 as a greenhouse gas. Since the industrial revolution, atmospheric ozone concentrations have increased by approximately 30%, making it the third most significant greenhouse gas after CO_2 and methane.

Sources and Sinks

Tropospheric ozone originates from the oxidation or breakdown of volatile organic compounds found in solvents like paints and hair sprays. Pollution from automobiles, industries, and fossil fuel burning increases carbon and nitrogen molecule concentrations in the lower atmosphere. These molecules react with sunlight to produce ozone. Ozone is primarily removed from the atmosphere through photochemical breakdown in sunlight.

Dangers

Tropospheric ozone poses significant health hazards to humans, animals, plants, and the environment. It can cause headaches, respiratory illnesses, and irritation to the eyes, nose, and throat, particularly for those with asthma and other respiratory diseases.

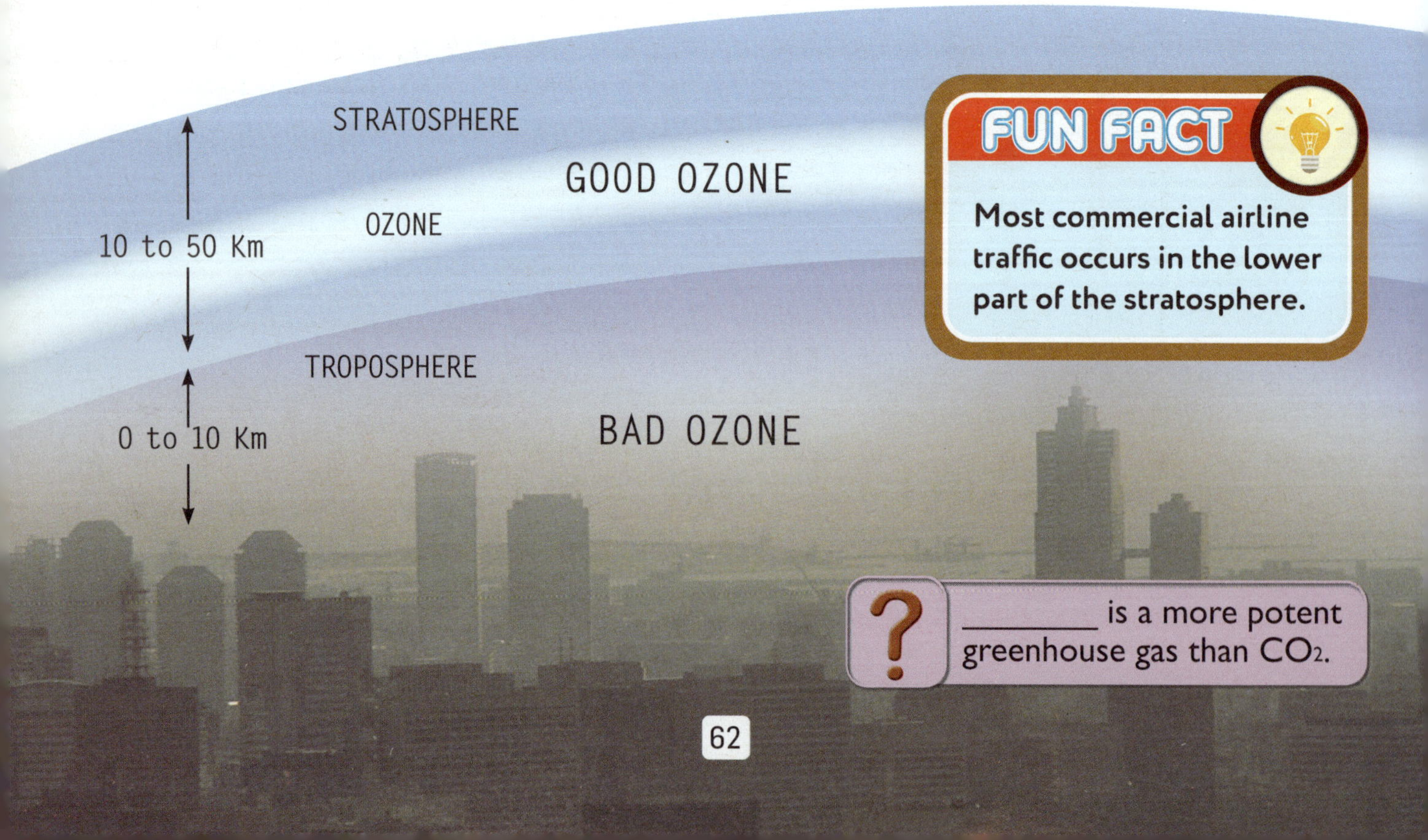

FUN FACT

Most commercial airline traffic occurs in the lower part of the stratosphere.

? ________ is a more potent greenhouse gas than CO_2.

Ozone Depletion

As CFCs and HCFCs reach the stratosphere, UV rays from the sun break them down, releasing chlorine atoms that react with ozone, initiating chemical cycles of ozone destruction. A single chlorine atom can break apart over 100,000 ozone molecules.

Antarctic Hole

Every spring, a hole forms over Antarctica, known as the Antarctic ozone hole. In 2000, it reached a record size, covering nearly 30 million square kilometers, roughly the size of the North American continent.

Aerosol spray cans contain CFCs which damaged the ozone layer

The Antarctic ozone hole

Plants and Animals

Harmful UV rays can penetrate water, posing a threat to aquatic organisms like plankton, which are essential for marine ecosystems. Plankton are particularly vulnerable to UV radiation, leading to their decline. As a key food source for many sea creatures, including whales, fish, and shrimp, a reduction in plankton population could push marine species towards extinction.

Arctic Hole

Smaller ozone holes also form annually over the Arctic, in the North Pole, permitting harmful UV light to reach populated areas in Europe. Ozone levels over the Northern Hemisphere have been declining by four percent per decade. Scientists predict that the ozone layer will be restored in the stratosphere by 2065.

FUN FACT

In 1987, the US and several other countries signed the Montreal Protocol treaty to phase out the production and use of ozone-depleting substances.

? When was the Montreal Protocol treaty signed? ________________

Kyoto Protocol

The Kyoto Protocol, adopted in December 1997 in Kyoto, Japan, aimed to combat the effects of human activities on the natural climate by regulating greenhouse gases. Over 190 countries have signed and ratified the protocol.

Targets

Under the protocol, each country commits to reducing its greenhouse gas emissions. The goal is to collectively cut total emissions by at least 5 percent by 2008-2012. The treaty targets the reduction of the six main greenhouse gases: carbon dioxide, methane, nitrous oxide, sulfur hexafluoride, HFCs, and PFCs.

Projects

Several initiatives and programmes were introduced globally to reduce greenhouse gas emissions. Countries like Italy shifted to renewable energy sources, while businesses initiated projects like tree planting and creating wind and solar energy facilities.

United States and Kyoto Protocol

The US, accounting for about one-fourth of the world's greenhouse gas emissions, initially withdrew its support for the Kyoto Protocol, citing concerns over high economic costs relative to benefits.

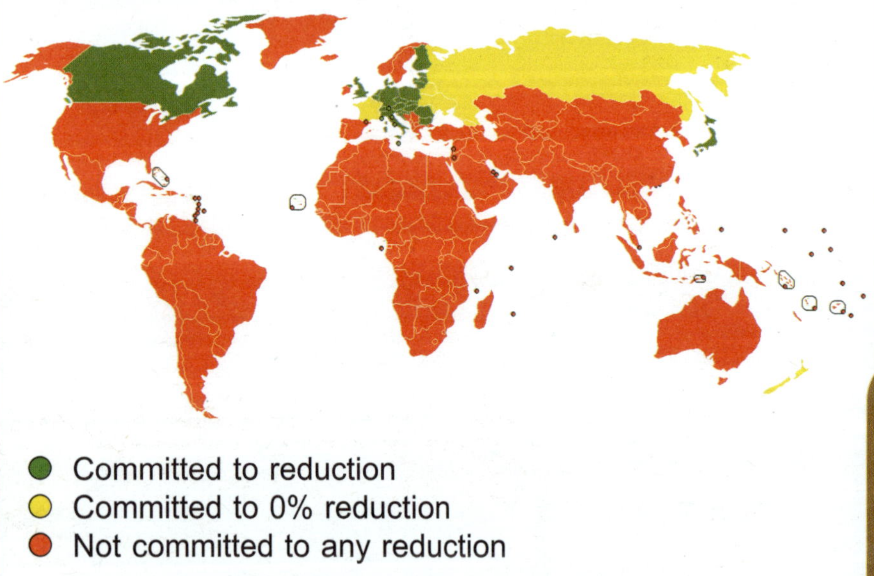

Map overview of countries committed to reduction of CO_2 emission in the 2008-2012 Kyoto period

FUN FACT

Under the Kyoto Protocol, low-emission countries like Iceland were allowed to maintain stable emission levels due to their smaller global contribution and unique circumstances.

? How many countries have signed and ratified the Kyoto Protocol? ____________

Food Waste

Food waste contributes to GHG emissions, particularly through methane emissions from rotting food in landfills. Certain foods have a greater impact on the atmosphere than others. For instance, research indicates that wasted milk in Britain emits 100,000 tonnes of CO_2 into the atmosphere annually.

Waste Food Emissions

Annually, approximately one-third or 1.43 billion tonnes of food produced globally for human consumption is wasted. This leads to over 135 million tonnes of GHG emissions annually, making up 1.5% of total emissions.

Reduce Food Waste

To reduce food waste, individuals should purchase only what they need and avoid leftovers when possible. If leftovers do occur, freezing them for later consumption is advisable. Additionally, food waste can be converted into compost for household plants and gardens.

Sources

Improper handling or storage of food during transportation can lead to wastage. In restaurants, inadequate training of food handlers contributes to this issue. In households, food spoilage and over-purchasing are major causes of waste. Commonly wasted vegetables include citrus fruits, cherries, sweet potatoes, green vegetables, and onions.

FUN FACT

350 million litres of milk is wasted annually.

How much food wastage occurs in the UK? ____________

Carbon Capture and Storage

CCS is a technology that captures CO_2 from fossil fuel power stations and transports it through pipelines to deep underground structures offshore, such as depleted oil and gas reservoirs and deep saline aquifers, where it is stored safely. This storage method helps mitigate global warming and climate change.

Carbon Sinks

Carbon is stored in four major reservoirs within the Earth. It's crucial to maintain carbon in these reservoirs to mitigate global warming:

1 Oceans: Carbon is present in oceans as dissolved CO_2 and in marine organisms, including their shells.

2 Living organisms: Plants absorb CO_2 and release oxygen during photosynthesis. Carbon is utilized in food production and transferred through the food chain.

3 Sediments: Carbon is stored in rocks, soil (like limestone), and fossil fuels like coal, oil, and gas.

4 Atmosphere: Carbon is found in the atmosphere as greenhouse gases, including CO_2, CH_4, CO, and chlorofluorocarbons.

Carbon Sources

Carbon enters the atmosphere through various means, including:

- Animal respiration
- Decomposition of organic matter
- Biomass combustion
- Industrial processes
- Volcanic eruptions
- Releases from permafrost
- Mining activities
- Forest fires

? The full form of CCS is ____________.

FUN FACT

By burning fossil fuels, we release stored carbon into the atmosphere.

Carbon Footprint

A carbon footprint is the total greenhouse gas emissions produced by an individual, business, or product. The per capita carbon footprint is highest in the United States. Individuals and organizations can help combat climate change by reducing their carbon footprint.

Carbon Offsets

A carbon offset is an activity that compensates for the emission of CO_2 and other greenhouse gases into the atmosphere. Examples include energy efficiency improvements such as installing energy-efficient light bulbs in homes and workplaces.

Insulating windows during winters can help save a lot of energy

Alternative Energy

The carbon footprint can be reduced by utilizing alternative energy sources such as wind, hydroelectric, and solar energy, which produce no carbon emissions. Additionally, purchasing energy-efficient and reusable goods helps minimize carbon dioxide and methane emissions. Furthermore, more efficient fuels are replacing fossil fuels.

Consumption

Burning fossil fuels for energy is a major cause of global warming. To reduce it, individuals can conserve energy by turning off appliances such as lights and computers when not in use. Vehicles also contribute to pollution, so carpooling and using public transportation can help reduce carbon footprint.

? Can the use of alternative energy reduce carbon footprint? ______

FUN FACT

GHGs are more effective at trapping heat higher up in the atmosphere where it is colder, compared to near the warm surface of the earth.

Effect on Mars and Venus

Mars and Venus, Earth's closest neighbors, share similarities in size and characteristics but do not support life. Venus is extremely hot, with surface temperatures akin to a furnace, while Mars is cold. Studying their atmospheres offers insights into potential climate changes on Earth.

Mars

Mars, known as the red planet, has a thin atmosphere, primarily composed of 95 percent CO_2, 3 percent nitrogen, and minimal water vapour. Its weak gravitational pull prevents effective heat retention, resulting in drastic temperature fluctuations between day and night. This leads to prolonged dust storms covering the planet. The cold atmosphere causes water to freeze in the poles and permafrost, reducing the greenhouse effect and fostering a colder climate. Unlike Earth, Mars lacks an ozone layer, leaving its surface vulnerable to harmful UV radiation, which erodes organic compounds.

Venus

Venus, the second planet from the sun, holds the distinction of being the hottest planet in the solar system, primarily due to an extensive greenhouse effect. Its atmosphere, composed predominantly of 96.5 percent CO_2, traps significant solar radiation, resulting in surface temperatures soaring up to 482° C. With minimal water and clouds mainly comprising sulfuric acid droplets, Venus experienced an initial warming phase that converted liquid water into water vapour, further exacerbating the greenhouse effect by releasing trapped CO_2 from rocks, thus intensifying the planet's carbon content.

FUN FACT

At night, the temperature of Mars can drop to -82° C.

? Which is the hottest planet in the solar system? ________

Glossary

Accumulation: the quantity of something that has increased over a period

Aerosol: a substance that is kept in a container under high pressure so that it can be sprayed

Anaerobic combustion: the process of burning without oxygen

Anthropogenic: pollutants generated by human activities

Biomass: animal dung and other animal waste used as a fuel

Compost: a mixture made by the decomposition of plant and vegetable waste, to add to soil

Deforestation: the process of cutting down a large number of trees

Ecosystem: a community of living organisms and their interaction with each other and their physical environment Such as air, water and soil

Eruption: to emit or discharge with a force

Euphoria: a feeling of intense happiness

Fermentation: the process of breakdown of the food by microorganisms such as yeast

Hydroelectric power: electricity generated with the power of flowing water

Industrial revolution: a period of development in industries, agriculture, textile and transportation

Inevitable: something that is impossible to prevent

Infrared: a type of light that can be felt as heat but cannot be seen

Insulation: protection from cold and heat

Magnitude: of great extent, importance

Permafrost: a subsurface layer of soil that remains frozen throughout the year, usually in the polar regions

Pesticide: a substance that is used to kill those insects that damage crops

Photochemical: a chemical reaction caused by light

Precipitation: water released from clouds as rain, snow, hail or sleet

Radiate: to emit energy in the form of rays, heat and waves

Ratify: to approve something by officially signing it

Reservoir: a large quantity of something that can be used anytime

Sedative: a medicinal drug that makes one fall asleep

Semiconductor: a solid substance that allows electricity to pass through it when its temperature increases

Smog: a mixture of smoke and fog in the atmosphere

Solvent: a substance which is capable of dissolving a solid substance

Stratosphere: a part of Earth's atmosphere that is 10-50 km above the surface

Sublimation: the process in which a solid substance changes into gas or vice versa without becoming liquid

Topography: the physical features of the earth such as mountains, hills, rivers, etc.

Transpiration: the process in which water from leaves passes into the atmosphere as water vapour

Volatile: any liquid or substance that can quickly change into gas

Wetland: an area of land fully or partially submerged in water

Answers

Page 51 - 31 percent
Page 52 - 30 degrees
Page 53 - About 80 million metric tonnes
Page 54 - Oxygen
Page 55 - True
Page 56 - Denitrification
Page 57 - 14-260 years
Page 58 - 17,200
Page 59 - True
Page 60 - 21.8 percent
Page 61 - Charles Fabry and Henri Buisson
Page 62 - Ozone
Page 63 - In 1987
Page 64 - 1990
Page 65 - Seven million tonnes
Page 66 - Carbon Capture and Storage
Page 67 - Yes
Page 68 - Venus

Notes

Notes